IF THE SKY WAS MY HEART

If the Sky Was My Heart

EDITOR
Blake More

ASSISTANT EDITOR
Emily Carr

FIELD EDITORS
Diana Hallare, Dan Levinson, and
Magdelena Montagne

Foreword by
Victoria Chang

CALIFORNIA POETS IN THE SCHOOLS
STATEWIDE ANTHOLOGY 2014

Printed in the United States of America

ISBN 978-0-939927-25-8

Design: Josef Beery
Cover art: Molly Mielke, Mendocino Grammar School

"One Day in Workshop," by Gabrielle LeMay, was first published in
Askew Poetry 15, Fall 2013/Winter 2014.

To order copies of *If the Sky Was My Heart,* please contact:

California Poets in the Schools
1333 Balboa Street, No. 3
San Francisco, CA 94118
(415) 221-4201
info@cpits.org
www.cpits.org

Heliotrope

for Susan Sibbet

See that spark of light
at the far edge of vision,
shining across the separating distance?

How it flies over the curve of the earth
like a dove making its own tiny dawn?

Someone is out there, straddling the horizon,
waiting for the shine of your mirror
to turn toward theirs.

This is the moment,
the signal you came here for.

Across the gulf, your own light answers.

The remoteness collapses,
becomes suddenly
nothing.

ARTHUR DAWSON
Poet-teacher, Sonoma County

*Note: A heliotrope, named after a flower that follows the sun, is
a mirrored survey tool that reflects the sun over long distances.*

Contents

DANCE OF THE RAINBOW

LEAF PORTAL

Foreword

"This / is / just / to / say / I / broke / your china vase, / but / I / had to / in order / to / kill / the bug / that / was crawling / on / it." This mostly one-word-per-line poem isn't found in *If the Sky Was My Heart*; it's a poem I wrote in fourth grade at Ealy Elementary in West Bloomfield, Michigan. I still have the nearly two-hundred-page spiral-bound book, handmade and hand-typed by teachers and volunteers thirty-three years ago. My poem and another one by me won "1 place" in a district-wide contest. After all of my twenty-plus moves around the country and the world, I still have this book, with its chocolate-brown cover and resumé-like paper.

As an adult poet and writer with a somewhat unusual background (I have an MBA in business as well as an MFA in poetry writing), I'm often asked, "When did you start writing poetry?" Like the young writers in *If the Sky Was My Heart*, I started at a very young age. And like many of these young writers, I didn't start writing on my own: teachers not only introduced me to poetry, they inspired me.

We received ribbons, apparently, which have since disappeared, but I will never lose my hand-bound book. Winning the award and having my two poems published in an anthology were important to me as a child, and I still remember feeling a great sense of pride. Seeing my poems in print not only inspired me to continue writing, it also made me feel suddenly worthy, as if what I had to say was actually important.

Growing up in the Midwest as the child of a Chinese American immigrant was challenging, and I often felt lost and trapped. Poetry was an escape for me, a way to use my imagination to articulate emotions I couldn't express in daily life. In today's high-pressure, media-filled, fast-paced world, poetry is a way for children to sit quietly and listen to words, to see images, and to think more deeply. Poetry is a chance for today's hyper-stimulated generation to just sit and think about the comma and the period, and the little hummingbird at work outside the window.

When I began to read the poems in *If the Sky Was My Heart,* I was immediately brought back to childhood and the wonder and anxiety I felt when I was the age of these student poets. Renee Cai, a fourth-grader, is just beginning to understand the paradoxes of life in her poem "House of Memory," where a sad memory "is coming through the door." The speaker in the poem, though, has self-determination and hope: "I will / put it in the Room of Opposites // where grass grows down / and roots reach the sun." What scope and imagination for a fourth-grader! This beautifully complex poem makes my poem about a broken vase and a fly seem overly simplistic.

What I love about the minds of young children is how they are so often filled with hope and optimism, as in first-grader Alisa Liao's poem "Ode to My Mom," where in seven short lines, Liao expresses deep love for her mother: "Your skin glows white like the moon on the darkest night," and "Your heart is much more smooth and soft than silk." Or as in second-grader Aditi Borra's poem "Big Sister," where she similarly expresses optimistic love but observantly notes her sister's worries: "She's an oak tree stretching out her worries. / She's a white pearl falling like rain." The poet's job is to see and observe, and Borra already has the mind and eye of a poet. Like Borra, fifth-grader Lucas Gaede understands the paradoxes of people. In "My Brother," he writes: "He is soft on the outside / and hard in the middle. / My brother is blurred, / but is sometimes as blazing / as the setting sun." These odes are impressive in their sophistication and multiple dimensions.

So many of the young poets in *If the Sky Was My Heart* employ sound and rhythm to bring life to their poems and to words that might otherwise be flat. Ninth-grader April Truong, in "Dance of the Rainbow," writes about the Thai countryside, drawing the reader in with the use of repetition and rhythmic language: "Every single drop of perspiration and blood / Dawn to dusk, dawn to dusk / The rhythm from the beat of dying hearts . . ." Later in the poem, we see the repetition: "Moving callously to every sound they played at me / Dusk to dawn, dusk to dawn . . ." But here, an inversion subtly creates tension. And later, more repetition in the form of anaphora: "In your heart you smell / The flame that now engulfs your sorrow," and "In your heart you see / The rainbow that still haunts your dreams."

Likewise, second-grader Marin Hereen, in "Noises at Dawn," seems to have a natural ear for language and sound: "At dawn the city rings / And dings and clinks / And clanks, from the bells / Ringing, children singing, / Mice are squeaking, / Foxes peeking, cats / Scurrying, bats are /

Hurrying, frogs jumping, / Raindrops plunking. . . ."
Hereen sounds like a young Gerard Manley Hopkins.

Despite the darkness in my own poems, many people who read them say that they are "funny," and when I do poetry readings, people often laugh at places I never expected them to laugh. Humor is something I love in poetry even though I don't use it intentionally. Fifth-grader August Independence Curtis Riehl, in his poem "California Is a Chicken Potpie," uses a clever and funny image: "I love California chicken potpie / it has a rich history of flavor. . . . // there's Los Angeles and the meat and potatoes of Hollywood / the homeland of entertainment / carrots like James Bond and Tron . . ."

One of my poetry teachers once said that poets seem to have an innate sense of metaphor, that they see the world in metaphor. I think, though, that metaphor can be taught, and clearly many of the student poets in *If the Sky Was My Heart* have been taught how to skillfully use metaphor by their poet-teachers. Fifth-grader Aeneas Nicholas, in his poem "Anger," sharply uses metaphor to express emotion: "Anger is a black hole far out in space / crushing everything that comes near it / and disregarding anything that tries to soothe its force. / Anger is a hurricane spinning and striking and / wrecking everything in its way. . . ." In the last line, Nicholas reveals his maturity and the paradoxical nature of anger when he writes: "Anger is tasteless."

Similarly, fifth-grader Emmanuel Tiscareno, in "Violence Road," uses metaphor to describe the gang-ridden landscape that he sees: "There is a road that no one's heard of but me,

/ a road that I call Violence Road. / I drive through this road. / I see gangs, broken TVs, and people fighting. // It's a road that everyone's afraid of / but me. A road that's killed millions, / even my great-grandpa. // It's a road that has history in everything. / I warn you all, so / stay out." Tiscareno describes an expansive violent history subtly, with an understanding that sometimes the most powerful forms of writing are the most understated.

Brinda Venkat, a second-grader, uses metaphor so strongly in her poem "Earth" that it could have been easily written by a person much older than she. Her vision is wide, and her mind travels far: "I am earth. I am a planet. / I have dirt below me. / If you go far, you will find mountains, / rocks, and volcanoes. // I am round. / Sometimes I am mucky. / If you go to space, / I look like a big blue clay ball."

Much of my poetry explores issues of identity, both ethnicity and gender. Jazz musician Vijay Iyer, in a speech to Yale University's Asian American alumni, said of his experience of being an Asian American: "It means that our lives here are characterized by a constant borderline status with respect to Americanness; we're always right on the frontier of what it means to be American." Eleventh-grader Kathy Orozco, in "*Sin Fronteras*," writes of sadness and of displacement in her native Spanish, translated by poet-teacher Jabez W. Churchill: "I'm from that place / so very far away / that it is difficult to get there, / but when I need to, / my heart and my soul / are capable of traveling there in seconds / and feeling the breeze / from that beach that I enjoyed so much. / My dreams have no borders. / My accomplishments, no end." The poem ends with a melancholy nostalgia: "I miss those afternoons that were a pleasure / when my mother used to chat with me / until the evening." This poem reminds me of Li-Young Lee's poems about his family in *The Rose*.

Identity isn't something that relates only to gender or ethnicity, though. In many ways, children of all ages are going through daily crises of identity simply because they are trying to make sense of the world around them. Fourth-grader Alicia Chen, in her poem "My Elements: Earth," understands that there are many sides to her, and in her poem struggles to make sense of them: "I shake like an earthquake, / I erupt like a volcano. / My outside is as hard as a rock. / My inside is soft, / a dark brown soil." She asks the reader to look deeper: "Don't judge on what you see outside, / look underground and deep, / look past that boulder, look past that mountain!"

To some extent, all of us, young and old, no matter where we are from, just want to be understood and accepted for who we are, not who we are expected to be. Eleventh-grader LaShanae Barnes writes a poetic anthem, "Who Do You Think I Am?" that expresses this precisely: "Being black, you might think / Oh yeah, she's loud, hangs out with / The wrong crowd and / She'll be pregnant before she's eighteen // But you don't even know me / To be judging me // I am smart, love to read / And I write poetry // But those are the things / You wouldn't see in a girl like me . . . // I'm just saying . . . let me do me." Barnes takes racial stereotypes and confronts them head-on with verve and zest.

When I first started reading the poems in *If the Sky Was My Heart*, I didn't know what to expect. But I was immediately riveted, charmed, and impressed by the heart, hope, skill, depth, and intelligence of these young poets. And I was even more heartened by the poems of the poet-teachers, many of which showed how much passion they have for teaching our children the mysteries and beauty of art. These poems awakened emotions I hadn't felt in a long time and give me great hope for the future, as second-grader Tiarri Washington so aptly writes: "In the poem of myself, / I see light / in the darkest cave, / hear a butterfly's wing beat, / feel the earth / around me."

—Victoria Chang

Editor's Note

This is an exceptional anthology in an exceptional year, for it's not often that a grassroots literary arts organization celebrates turning fifty. While the word *grassroots* may seem like a misnomer to some, California Poets in the Schools would not exist if it weren't for the hundreds, even thousands, of poets who answered yes to the call to share the love of expression and the power of words with California youth. From San Diego to Del Norte, we currently have 123 active poet-teachers devotedly cultivating children's creativity through poetry and performance.

Of course, such statewide presence would be impossible without the dedicated staff working hours beyond pay in our San Francisco office to make sure that poet-teachers, their students, and their schools are supported in these efforts. We are truly a team, and like all hard-working, effective teams, we must occasionally take a moment to step back and take a bow. A bow to ourselves; to the poets of the past whose shoulders we stand on; to the students of today who are learning to paint with words, invent new language, express ideas, and break the rules of punctuation and grammar; to the youth who found us as adults and became poet-teachers themselves; and finally to everyone—schools, administrators, parents, funders, poets, teachers, city councils, newspapers, graphic designers, editors—who has made the California Poets in the Schools literary legacy a lasting one.

So, I invite you—yes, you, the very you reading this sentence right now—to pause for a moment and acknowledge that we are here—doggedly perched upon the milestone of a half century. Wow. Doesn't that feel like seeds being watered and rivers winding into ocean? Oh, if the sky was my heart!

Yes. Here. Once again celebrating language with a collection of poems from up and down the state, carefully selected from hundreds of submissions by the team of editors tasked with this difficult responsibility—Dan Levinson, Diana Hallare, Magdalena Montagne, Emily Carr, and myself—and joined in this delightful anthology of voices.

Imagine, if the sky were everyone's heart. It would be like this anthology: a message of resilience, fortitude, and hope; of family and love; a steadfast realization that California's youth have the power within to make themselves into what they want, to ensure that dreams come true, to forge peace and clarity in these confusing times.

Eighth-grader Julia Nacario asks, "Can your one voice be heard / over a million strong?" High-schooler Kathy Orozco tells us: "My dreams have no borders. / My accomplishments, no end." Freshman Kirsten Ikehara wants "to be an original, / The book in a room of Kindles. // I want to last, / My well-worn pages here until you can't read my words. // I want to make an impression, / Staying in your mind, / Not coming out the other side."

These works, and many others in this collection, express a strong notion of self and take you on a journey through a path of the mind and heart, the soul and the body, leading to a destination even the authors cannot foresee—just like life. So as California Poets in the Schools enters its golden years, let us pledge to continue to encourage youth and their poet-teachers to forge new pathways of creative expression and give voice to the unmapped depths of growth and inquiry. Let us feel the magic, and let our thoughts soar skyward with the imagination of poetry, where—in the words of fourth-grader Renee Cai—grass "grows down / and roots reach the sun."

—Blake More

Dream
Conversations

Dream Conversations

"Look," I said in one dream.
"See," I said in another.
The rain came down.
The stars rose up.
Everything fell.
The trees swayed in the wind,
She jumped with joy,
She sat with sadness.
Overall, dreams that you dream
are always worth dreaming.

ELLA JOHNSTON
Grade Four, Springhill School, Alameda County
Debbie Deitch, classroom teacher
J. Ruth Gendler, poet-teacher

Small

Small is a single raindrop from the dark
rainstorm. Small, a pinch of light and hope
shining into a dark prison cell. Small, a chick
putting all its trust into its shining mother.
Small, a single note that gets famous.
A small sparkle of magic in a witch's hat.
Small, a piece of sun coming down
on the sparkling snow, and then it disappears.
Small.

MIA SANDERS
Grade Three, Montecito Union Elementary, Santa Barbara County
Connie Maday, classroom teacher
Christine Kravetz, poet-teacher

Why Movement?

Is movement just your legs carrying you,
or are you tackling your way into life?
Are you launching for the emeralds,
or are you moving your hands
in such a way that it mesmerizes the crowd?
Or are you the flame flickering too fast to see?
Could you be the slowest one of all
        or the lightning?

RYAN MURGATROYD
Grade Six, Kenwood Elementary School, Sonoma County
Jane Springer, classroom teacher
Arthur Dawson, poet-teacher

The Holdfast

Child, don't
grow roots
around spent shells or
piddling stones. Fasten
yourself to a rock, at
home on the bottom
with monsters and
silence.
Forgive
its
sadness,
its
traffic
with
death.
An
old
stone
that
rode
volcanoes,
tidal
waves,
earth's
shifts
around
the

core

will

not

budge when

waves and currents

heave, except to save you.

That since its exploding birth

never felt sun on its pebbled skin,

yet holds fast in the dark deep

while you grow into the light.

GWYNN O'GARA
Poet-teacher, Sonoma County

House of Memory

In the House of Memory, I see
through the window of nothingness.

I am part of your brain, and
I am here to help you, but

I don't create your memory—
you create it.

Look, a memory
is coming through the door,

but it is a sad memory. I will
put it in the Room of Opposites

where grass grows down
and roots reach the sun.

RENEE CAI
Grade Four, Spreckels School, San Diego County
Elizabeth Stewart, classroom teacher
Seretta Martin, poet-teacher

The Dream

After Emily Dickinson

A tiger's like a dream I had.
It comes out of nowhere.
It takes a sip of water
and goes to the den of dreams.

A shadow is like a rude kid
that copies your every step.
It plays shadow tag until it can't,
because I do not move.

GAVIN ROGNLIEN
Grade Three, Prestwood School, Sonoma County
Carly Talesfore-Costello, classroom teacher
Phyllis Meshulam, poet-teacher

After Lisel Mueller's "Imaginary Paintings"

How I would paint amnesia
An unknown attic
rustling with the wind,
broken stairs
croaking with every step,
eerie darkness with ominous lights.
Out-of-place grandfather clocks
ticking randomly,
forgotten children
crying out for their mama.
A dark cemetery,
glowing with a single wax candle.

How I would paint fear
A lonely scorpion
gnawing its way through your shoe.
Approaching certain death.
A graveyard smeared with the blood of fallen enemies.
A cloud of fog
approaching with sluggish speed.
A murder of crows
gliding their way toward you.

How I would paint catastrophe
A tornado blowing away a red farm.
Your child's playhouse
stacked with garbage.
Termites devouring their way effortlessly
through your moldy, decaying wood.
A light flickering in the gloomy closet,
now just piles of meaningless glass.

JORDAN WESTOVER
Grade Eight, St. Thomas the Apostle, San Francisco County
Laura Fracchia-Riviello, classroom teacher
Florencia Milito, poet-teacher

The Origin of a Piano

A bang of the left hand
Got the right hand singing

The immense creativity
That differed the white plump key
From the skinny black one awed me so

Like a lady planting flowers
Row by row by row
In pattern
With exquisite care

And the flowers danced
The right hand sang
And she captured this moment

With a whisk of her hand
And
The piano was born

SIERRA SABEC
Grade Six, Lagunitas School, Marin County
Laurie Riley, classroom teacher
Brian Kirven, poet-teacher

After Neruda's Book of Questions

Does a drop of water
know it's a part of a river?

Can your one voice be heard
over a million strong?

Is the tree tall enough
to touch the sky?

What whimsical surprise lies
at the colorful rainbow's end?

How many flavors
are there of wild berries?

Is the raven nothing but a
shadow in the dead of night?

How far can the roars
of twenty tigers be heard?

Why aren't fish called alcoholics
when they drink so much?

How do gophers navigate
their dusty underground homes?

Where lies the secret
of the oyster's pearl?

JULIA NACARIO
Grade Eight, St. Thomas the Apostle, San Francisco County
Laura Fracchia-Riviello, classroom teacher
Florencia Milito, poet-teacher

After Passing Through the Gate at Tiahuanacu

I used to be a man
Now I am a moon in shadow
Patiently waiting for the sun to rise

I used to be your teacher
Now I am the song
Your grandchild sings at dawn
While she paints a picture of you
Smiling

JIM CARTWRIGHT
Poet-teacher, San Francisco County

Dawn

Dawn

After Sappho

A moment ago, gold-sandaled
dawn woke me up with
the voice of my mom.
She tells me to wake up
or the bus will leave me.
I get dressed and I put
on my golden-winged
sandals. I brush
my teeth and then
I grab my backpack
and go flying to
the bus stop.

EDUARDO LOPEZ
Grade Six, Cali Calmécac Language Academy, Sonoma County
Richard Meza, classroom teacher
Phyllis Meshulam, poet-teacher

Ode to My Mom

Your voice is like an angel singing under silver bells.
Your skin glows white like the moon on the darkest night.
You are sweeter than caramel-filled chocolate.
Your hair curls are like waves rolling in the ocean.
Your eyes sparkle like the sun in the afternoon.
Your clothes are as pretty as petunia flowers.
Your heart is much more smooth and soft than silk.

ALISA LIAO
Grade One, Gomes Elementary, Alameda County
Mrs. Barcelos, classroom teacher
Mara Sheade, poet-teacher

Big Sister

She's an oak tree stretching out her worries.
She's a white pearl falling like rain.
She's a little kitten crawling around the house,
a baby in a tiny cradle.
A gymnast by word,
she's a rose that blooms everywhere,
a sun that shines every time.
She's my big sister.

ADITI BORRA
Grade Two, John Gomes Elementary School, Fremont, Alameda County
Mr. Muck, classroom teacher
Cathy Barber, poet-teacher

My Brother

I recognize the past
as if it is my brother.
I remember hiking up
the hills and in the valleys,
and squirrels chuckling
in the treetops of the gnarled
bark of the pines. Fishing
from afternoon to dusk
with my brother. My brother
is good at fishing and is like
moss growing on a tree.
He is soft on the outside
and hard in the middle.
My brother is blurred,
but is sometimes as blazing
as the setting sun.

LUCAS GAEDE
Grade Five, Washington Elementary School, Santa Barbara County
Sara Barr, classroom teacher
Kyli Larson, poet-teacher

Untitled

He's a ripe peach.
He's a pair of shoes
resting on a sofa.
He's a little fire
burning on the stove.
He's a candy wrapper
flying in the wind.
He's as playful
as a bouncy ball.
He's a flying rocket
taking off.
If placed in a car,
off he goes
in the fire-lit sky.

KRISHNA JAMAKHANDI
Grade Two, John Gomes Elementary School, Fremont, Alameda County
Mrs. Essex, classroom teacher
Cathy Barber, poet-teacher

My Father's Hands

Scarred are my father's
hands and wrists
from cuts,
never self-inflicted,
but the scars
of a working man.
Unfortunately, also those
of a junkie,
the poison needle
long gone,
but its marks
ever present,
the veins standing out.
He wears fantastic
silver bracelets,
drawing attention away
from the marks.
I think he's ashamed,
embarrassed,
or both.

The hands of my father,
loving and caring,
despite the permanent marks
and the roughness.

CASSIDY BAILEY
Grade Nine, Six Rivers Charter School, Humboldt County
Meghan Froloff, classroom teacher
Julie Hochfeld, poet-teacher

Kindling

There was a time when the fall
was punctuated with stacking firewood.
My grandmother at the cross sawhorse,
& me, a child stacking cords of wood
against the shingled wall of the shed.
She showed me how to wedge the ends
with split wood to make a jigsaw puzzle.
When she sawed through the sawhorse,
we changed jobs: I sawed, she stacked.
Each year, she moved a little slower,
while I became expert at greasing
bow-saw blades too precious to snap.
The saw bit into sunlit sawdust, an acrid legacy.
The axe & wedge split the secret heartwood.
Over the years, we built great cord walls
that could stretch to China, or the moon.
Nothing was wasted. Mulched leaves
kept the garden warm. Without kindling,
the sap from the oak & bay wouldn't bleed
& sing of secret aquifers, or cry of old storms.
They'd gurgle & hiss in dark-sooted tongues
and then flood the house with smoke.
So we coaxed their gift of heat & light
with small scraps from the woodpile.
Impatient, I stomped on a green bay branch
to break it in two for kindling, but the tip
lashed back to pierce my upper lip.
Two inches away from blindness

I was, that day.   A font of blood
bathed my teeth in metallic sacrifice.
I was a big girl, so I swallowed
back the tears, and stacked wood
for the coming winter.

MAUREEN HURLEY
Poet-teacher, Alameda County

My House

The couch all squishy feeling good.
The squeaky door of the shed is like a shriek.
I hear the fire siren of my sister jumping
on the trampoline. A mermaid's tail through the water,
and the tail scraping against a seashell
of my father washing the dishes, my mother
washing clothes, a shark's fin out of water.
The natural pathway of the earth and the trees
swaying like the slushy sound of sucking on a yogurt
tube. The madness of the tetherball getting stuck on the tree.
The soft silk of my bed like drifting or sinking through water.
The maze of the rug, and there's another dead end.
The lemons falling off the tree like the pick of my nail.
As for me and my house, the beauty keeps on.

STELLA BECIR
Grade Four, Marquez Charter Elementary, Los Angeles County
Clare Gardner, classroom teacher
Michelle Bitting, poet-teacher

Dance
of the Rainbow

Dance of the Rainbow

Endlessly sprawling horizon of rice paddies
Deep, lush green mountain forestry
Surrounding the rural Thai countryside
Children untouched by worry and frustration
Chasing tangible tadpoles in rivers
Ignoring the minnows that bit at their tiny toes
Falling down like a gentle spring shower
Drops of rainbows that danced

It started when they buried into the clouds
Rivers dryer than the sun's grace
Raucous pattering of feet and laughter
Gone as the winds that never came
Sickened from the taste of parched dirt
Tired of putting out the blaze that would not stop
Weary of shaking out the dust that does not want to settle
Devoid of rice wine to pass around

My parents and my parents' parents
And their parents' parents
Toiling over this land that greedily swallows
Every single drop of perspiration and blood
Dawn to dusk, dawn to dusk
The rhythm from the beat of dying hearts
Harmonizing with my silent wails
That echo through this barren valley

My mother used to say that
People left the land in many ways
The pretty birds would take them, she would say
Or maybe they wanted to be closer to home
And decided to become the flowers
That cradle the Earth like a small child
Was it right for me to assume that
You had to be dead to leave

They whisked me off just as the moon rose
Gagged, tied up and carried off
Like I was a package ready to be shipped
For I was sold like a horse to entertain drunkards and lonely men
And I danced and whirled and softly cried
Moving callously to every sound they played at me
Dusk to dawn, dusk to dawn
Grimy worthless pennies thrown at my feet

Soon I became fearful and afraid
Not because one day I would end up
In the hands of a violent pig
But because I would forget
Forget the singing cochoas hiding in canopies
Forget the scent of mud after a monsoon
Forget the shape of my baby brother's hand in mine
Forget the sweet taste of mangos by the river

No place to hide, no place to go
You never realize you are alone
Until inside your heart you hear
The music that is playing to no one
In your heart you smell
The flame that now engulfs your sorrow
In your heart you see
The rainbow that still haunts your dreams

APRIL TRUONG
Grade Nine, Lowell High School, San Francisco County
Tim Lamarre, classroom teacher
Susan Terence, poet-teacher

Noises at Dawn

At dawn the city rings
And dings and clinks
And clanks, from the bells
Ringing, children singing,
Mice are squeaking,
Foxes peeking, cats
Scurrying, bats are
Hurrying, frogs jumping,
Raindrops plunking.
When I hear all those
Noises I know that I am
At home.

MARIN HEREEN
Grade Two, Hammer Montessori School, San Benito County
Christine Hoerbelt, classroom teacher
Amanda Chiado, poet-teacher

California Is a Chicken Potpie

I love California chicken potpie
it has a rich history of flavor
full of gold nuggets and rivers of gravy and Sierra Mountains
   of dough
that brought people from all over the globe
to try our tasty pie

there's Los Angeles and the meat and potatoes of Hollywood
the homeland of entertainment
carrots like James Bond and Tron
plus ventriloquists like Jeff Dunham
magicians, actors, comedians, dancers, rock stars
they add nutrition and hours of zest

then, there is the evolution of Silicon Valley
tech boy and girl heaven
computers, WiFi, Skype, Facebook
are what cooks the pie
makes mouths water with science and potatoes of possibility

of course, there are questionable people
who see a Loch Ness–like monster in the SF Bay
something that eats seals and growls at people
   while they are drinking their coffee
I'm not sure if that belongs in the pie
but maybe at Burning Man
with the artists who make imaginative sculptures
and wear extraordinary outfits

I don't know what Burning Man is like
but I'll bet it's the juicy creamy part of the pie
that I hope to sample when I'm twenty

but nothing tastes like our pie
the Point Arena potpie
junk beach the monument to our past
sunsets, seafood, stars
the low-calorie superfood ingredients
of this tiny city of freedom and community

some pies are turkey flavor,
not so much the real thing
like the ones in the cities
whose buildings are so bright they cover the night sky
but not ours, real chicken flavor
like the eggs at our local co-op
and the chunks of real meat
that we eat because everyone knows each other
and most people like each other
and respect each other
and are kind to each other

we can skateboard anywhere we want
and we can take a picture of our lighthouse
long after the tourists go home
plus no security cameras,
and we say hi to each other at the post office

everyone here has independence and some kind of spirituality
because Point Arena is as big in nature
as it is small in population

friends and family are the outside crusty part
   of my California pie
sometimes they are harder to chew than the other parts
but their texture is worth the effort

California potpie keeps me warm
I eat it in a bowl of freedom and flavor
if you too take a second to bake it carefully
you too will figure out how good it tastes

AUGUST INDEPENDENCE CURTIS RIEHL
Grade Five, Pacific Community Charter School, Mendocino County
Jef Schultz, classroom teacher
Blake More, poet-teacher

Pink

The pink balloon floats
       full,
       explodes.
The body is limber
       in the atmospheric
       odds. The pink
is against me.
       A pink flamingo
       lifts its leg
when it needs.
       They say we need to
       get rid of pink.
It is a kind of prison,
       prism of delicate justice.
       Pink is an invitation,
a mouth of memory,
       a time of Eden.
       Children's fingers stain
pink as they crumble, color
       the eggs. The pink
       always wants to leave,
but softness clings.
       Pink dares, its demise
       is red.
The universe sleeps pink,
       a snake in the grass.
       When he smiles I'm the pink

anticipation. The bees
           are flooding the garden, a war
           of pink. Nectar hands.
The underside of the body
           is a hue, a hive, birds
           whisper tricks,
a hatching of mystery, cool finger
           on a warm trigger.
           A handle, mother of pearl
palms pink with destruction.
Cool pink sunrise,
           things to come.

AMANDA CHIADO
Poet-teacher, San Benito County

Anger

Anger is a black hole far out in space
crushing everything that comes near it
and disregarding anything that tries to soothe its force.
Anger is a hurricane spinning and striking and
wrecking everything in its way.
Anger is like a triangle
with three stages to it.
Pain, your brain shuts down
then your heart beats faster.
Anger is a monster truck
smashing things for self-satisfaction.
Anger is a black wolf
hiding in the darkness
hunting you down.
Anger is a blood red clouding your vision.
Anger is a juicy steak taken from a recently
slaughtered cow. Anger is a stream breaking
the silence of sadness. Anger is throwing
something across the room.
Anger is tasteless.

AENEAS NICHOLAS
Grade Five, Park School, Marin County
Andrea Dunn, classroom teacher
Claire Blotter, poet-teacher

Violence Road

There is a road that no one's heard of but me,
a road that I call Violence Road.
I drive through this road.
I see gangs, broken TVs, and people fighting.

It's a road that everyone's afraid of
but me. A road that's killed millions,
even my great-grandpa.

It's a road that has history in everything.
I warn you all, so
       stay out.

EMMANUEL TISCARENO
Grade Five, Dana Gray Elementary, Mendocino County
Sally Miller, classroom teacher
Karen Lewis, poet-teacher

Immortality

For Nelson Mandela, 1918–2013

I remember . . . the day you earned your wings
To think you were immortal
As if you walked through a regenerating portal
Memories of you swirled
Apartheid, hate, and little passports
Protests, treason, and trial courts
Twenty-seven years of oppression and you even built
    tennis courts
Words, your bullets
Lips, a trigger
You were the rigger
Without you, black South Africans
Didn't have the courage to feel bigger
For this reason they charged you
With treason and they took you away
You didn't resist, you said okay
Person, prisoner, and president
Palace and tenement
A hero
An inspiration
To white and black
I think, I was right,

Willing to fight for what is right is undying,
Always remember . . .
"We must use time wisely and forever realize
That the time is always ripe to do right."

ANAIS NAGLE
Grade Eight, West Marin School, Marin County
Julie Cassel, classroom teacher
Brian Kirven, poet-teacher

Sin Fronteras

Soy de donde canta el mariachi
y la tequila hace más fuertes las notas.
Soy de aquel lugar tan lejos
que es difícil llegar en transporte
pero al sentir esa necesidad de estar allá
mi corazón y mi alma son capaces
de viajar en segundos
y sentir la brisa de aquella playa
a la que tanto disfruté.
Mis sueños no tienen fronteras.
Mis logros no tendrán fin.
Estoy en un país en él que es difícil vivir.
Pero vale la pena seguir.
Extraño aquellas tardes
cuales eran un placer
que mi madre platicaba conmigo
hasta el atardecer.

Without Borders

I'm from where the mariachi sing
and the tequila makes the notes stronger.
I'm from that place
so very far away
that it is difficult to get there,
but when I need to,
my heart and my soul

are capable of traveling there in seconds
and feeling the breeze
from that beach that I enjoyed so much.
My dreams have no borders.
My accomplishments, no end.
I'm in a country where it's difficult to live
but worth it to keep trying.
I miss those afternoons that were a pleasure
when my mother used to chat with me
until the evening.

KATHY OROZCO
Grade Eleven, Anderson Valley High School, Mendocino County
Amber Mesa, classroom teacher
Jabez W. Churchill, poet-teacher
(Translated by Jabez.W. Churchill)

Have a Day

of sweet nonsense
all your As and A+s
out the window
your *shoulds* collapsed
giggling on the grass
your *musts* in a tickle fight
with your *mustn'ts*

Have a day following
the blue dragonfly
of freedom, spreading
your own gossamer wings,
a day recalling the giggles
of your childhood, sliding
down slick banisters,
leaping stairs by threes

Have a day diving
into piles of autumn leaves
stomping your feet
in muddy puddles
painting your toenails
neon green

What I mean to say is
Have a day!

LOIS KLEIN
Poet-teacher, Santa Barbara County

Leaf
Portal

Leaf Portal

At night the leaf is a portal
with dust as mountains
droplets of water as rivers
When the leaf falls it is chaos
The portal of the leaf breaks apart
and the dimension dies

HIROKI COYLE
Grade Five, West Marin School, Marin County
Esther Underwood, classroom teacher
Brian Kirven, poet-teacher

The Flickering Cosmos

The darkness overwhelms
It glows
Fades, then shines again
Pulsing a rhythmic cycle
Red, then orange then red again
Staining the ebony sky scarlet
Forcing the night away
Then letting it return
Repeating itself over and over
Then, stronger than ever
The red light turns ivory
Searing the cold dark sky
Then it's gone
And the night returns
As strong as ever

NOAH LABER

Grade Six, Cabrillo Middle School, Ventura County
Anne Morningstar, classroom teacher
Tree Bernstein, poet-teacher

Narcissus

At three they laughed at my saying
"wose" for "rose" as they encircled
over and over watching my failed
round mouth   my sincerest efforts
to speak the unspeakable bloom—
Later, periwinkles grew in the desert of my
heart, little pink sturdy flowers pushing up
slowly   but the deepest garden harbored
bluebells   delicate   dangling on thin
stems   birds of their own feathers   and, then, fox-
gloves, mysterious fairy trumpets blaring their
speckled silent songs   and finally, that one
lone narcissus rich perfumy   filled with itself
whispering, "Sing for yourself,   the sweetest
song of all."

CLAIRE BLOTTER
Poet-teacher, Marin County

Guatemala Bella

Yo recuerdo que íbamos a buscar cherisco
bajo de las montañas para encender el fuego
Yo recuerdo que yo iba a la escuela a pie en las montañas
donde había vereda y regresaba a pie

Aquí es diferente que allá
Porque aquí los perros tienen donde dormir
Les compran comida
Allá a los perros les dan tamalitos en el suelo
Yellos duermen afuera en el frío

Beautiful Guatemala

I remember when we went to look for kindling
Below the mountains so we could make a fire
I remember when I went to school on foot in the mountains
There was a path and I also had to return on foot

Here it's different from there
because dogs have a place to sleep
And people buy them food
There, they give them tamalitos on the ground
And they sleep outside in the cold

BRENDA BAMACA
Grade Five, Mission Education Center, San Francisco County
Lily Chow, classroom teacher
Jim Cartwright, poet-teacher

White

a pearl in a delicate seashell
clouds that you gaze at
paper you write your thoughts on
the sound of freedom
cracking of icebergs
snow pouring from the endless sky
feels like the thick and runny glue
the happiness we share
the rough surface of the moon

AUDREY XIAO
Grade Six, Gomes Elementary, Alameda County
Ms. Ackerman, classroom teacher
Mara Sheade, poet-teacher

Rain

The rain
is like millions of bombs
falling from the sky.
I cannot escape
this giant battlefield.
    I am only safe
when shields of cloth
are above my head.
    There is not
a sprout of fire anywhere.
Water almost outranks
    everything.

NICHOLAS VOEGELS
Grade Four, Kenwood Elementary School, Sonoma County
Jennifer Creeth, classroom teacher
Arthur Dawson, poet-teacher

My Elements: Earth

I shake like an earthquake,
I erupt like a volcano.
My outside is as hard as a rock.
My inside is soft,
a dark brown soil.
Inside, I have peace,
hills, fields, and valleys.
Don't judge on what you see outside,
look underground and deep,
look past that boulder, look past that mountain!
Behind them grows peace.
Mounds of green, birds are free!
My soft, underground soil
is better on the inside.
Outside, I am hard,
boulder, grime, and rocks.
When I'm mad, I'm a volcano,
when I'm mad, I'm an earthquake.
Outside, there's mud, muck, and dirt.
Two completely different sides.
Please don't judge on what you see.
Both sides of me bring all my harmony.

ALICIA CHEN
Grade Four, Gomes Elementary School, Alameda County
Mrs. Simon, classroom teacher
Jennifer Swanton Brown, poet-teacher

Amber

I am amber
from a special kind of tree
in the tropics.
I ooze a very sticky sap,
like rubber trees leak rubber.
I pour down the trunk of the tree
like a raindrop sliding down a blade of grass.
My goop catches bugs and twigs
like a Venus flytrap tricks a fly into its lair.
I even trap creatures
like an avalanche that buries a pine tree
and a tidal wave that covers an island.
When I harden I'm a gemstone
that shines like gold
in a cave full of diamonds.

MUSTAFE HASSAN
Grade Four, Washington Carver Elementary, San Diego County
Bill McClain, classroom teacher
Claudia Poquoc, poet-teacher

Black Rosemary

Black stars
against the bright background
The plants spread wide
on the wall of the world
The green grass ruffles in the wind
The black rosemary
no one dares approach
The smell so sweet it's hard
not to touch
as it drifts through the breeze
on the quiet summer night

MADELEINE SHEA GERSON
Grade Five, Delphian Academy, Los Angeles County
Shannon McKernan, classroom teacher
Alice Pero, poet-teacher

Rainy Cloudy Crazy Day

Really tiny microscopic molecules live inside the rain
thunder lives inside the rain too, and clouds and cats and dogs
rain feels like nothing, or a shower
with a lot of water and a little
the rain has a brain that thinks about lightning
it is so big that it is bigger than five hundred
    fifty-five thousand schools
rain smells fresh like earth soup
and a smiley face on top of the notebook
rain sounds like daffodils on a beautiful day
like little drums tapping on the ground
like a tree branch growing
rain tastes like a cool glass of spring water
like hot chocolate by the fireplace
and a sunny smile and tacos with my family
rain looks like an owl falling to the ground
a car tire going really fast
a rose petal dropping from rosebush
the rain offers water for every animal, flower, person
so all can survive
really tiny microscopic molecules live inside the rain

K–2 CLASS
Fort Ross School, Sonoma County
Elizabeth Weiss, classroom teacher
Blake More, poet-teacher

Earth

I am earth.
I have green grass.
If people jump,
I pull them down with gravity.
I have stars above me filling the night sky.

I am earth. I am a planet.
I have dirt below me.
If you go far, you will find mountains,
rocks, and volcanoes.

I am round.
Sometimes I am mucky.
If you go to space,
I look like a big blue clay ball.

I am filled with diamonds.
When there is an earthquake,
I spread around ash.

I have hills.
I am spinning around the moon.
I have potholes when I want to make geysers.

I have rich soil. Plants grow on me.
I have precious flowers and
animals in the valley.
My sun warms me up.

The dust and grime of the universe made me.
People entertain themselves on me.
The sun scorches my surface.
I am constant.

BRINDA VENKAT
Grade Two, John Gomes Elementary School, Fremont, Alameda County
Ms. Udelhoven, classroom teacher
Cathy Barber, poet-teacher

The Essence of Mankind

The fresh mountain air
Is fading away
The big oak trees
Are fading away
Meadows of grass
Are fading away
Endangered animals
Are fading away
Our good decisions
Are fading away
Our loyalty
Is fading away
Our curiosity for the world
Is fading away
And one day, we will too.

ANGEL SANDOVAL
Grade Six, Hamilton School, Marin County
Tanya Madison, classroom teacher
Terri Glass, poet-teacher

Light Nougat

It is January when I bite into the sky
and taste sunset
the deep orange meal
draped with locks of lilac
blooming as if summer were here already
ribbons of hot pink edged in tiny bows of yellow
cobalt embracing them all

the hues mingle with the joy
I drank from your eyes this morning
knowing somewhere
you too bask in the last remaining liquid of this day

I quietly sing to the tiny things that make life vast
inhale the light skipping along the waterline
stop to palm flecks of abalone
keeping only the smallest
lest my pockets be too heavy
for pirouettes to carry me
wildly counting
one-two-three-four-nine-ten
past the heron posing amidst the clatter of gulls

a black Lab races from shore to lavender froth in tireless laps
seal pup bobbing and rolling and taunting just out of reach
rubber-booted photographers balance beside round rock
cameras, like me, aim to capture echoes of dusk

the sun steeps past the faraway ledge

steadfast on its path of day breaks

as beauty seeps down my cheeks

a tributary of blessings

this moment, the air

my lungs expanding

past the boundary of skin

the ocean exhaling me

in the enormity

of us all

BLAKE MORE
Poet-teacher, Mendocino County

Ode to the World

Like a cage keeping us people from danger.
The world is a dark cave waiting to be discovered.
Ode to the world, like the scent of roses in a flowery
garden. Ode to earth for letting the adventure animals
swing through the dangerous forest. Ode to the people
that walk on earth. Ode to all the fruit that keeps me alive
to write this poem. Think of all the life of earth as leaves
swinging on a lively tree. This world is a poem being written.
The world is sweet as a watermelon, but also a sour lemon.
The earth is a blue bubble full of good memories that's being
blown away from an unhappy person. The world is a book
being opened. Our world is an ocean crashing on a rocky
shore. Ode to all the things that earth lets us do. Most of
all, best of all, ode to the world for life.

AVA VENKOV
Grade Three, Marquez Charter Elementary, Los Angeles County
Susan Schwartz-Lack, classroom teacher
Michelle Bitting, poet-teacher

Instead

Instead of certainty, magpies
Instead of sunlight on the water, tears
Instead of hurry, a speckled egg
Instead of worry, the autumn lake
Instead of bitterness, soup
Instead of money, rain
Instead of hope, trust
Instead of blame, laundry on a line—
  a jitterbug of pant legs and sleeves

PRARTHO SERENO
Poet-teacher, Marin County

If the Sky Was My Heart

If the sky was my heart
the birds would be my voice.
If the river could talk
it would tell me to swim
until the end of time.
If the wind was my breath
the sky would be my soul.
If our galaxy was a rollercoaster
there would be a line
running through the Milky Way.
If I was the sun
I would be the king of light.
If my heart were the world
it would be filled with love.

EMILY MOZZETTI
Grade Four, Buri Buri Elementary School, South San Francisco
Ms. Moussa, classroom teacher
Maureen Hurley, poet-teacher

In the Poem
of Myself

In the Poem of Myself

In the poem of myself,
I see light
in the darkest cave,
hear a butterfly's
wing beat,
feel the earth
around me.

TIARRI WASHINGTON

Grade Two, Lakeshore Elementary School, San Francisco County
Oliver Glover, classroom teacher
Susan Terence, poet-teacher

Getting the Second-Graders' Attention

I begin with the word *explosion*,
then compare it to the color of a sunrise.
With this, our blast-off begins.
Their classroom, a solar-powered craft;
the hallway, a streak of blazing heat.
Don't avert your eyes, I advise.
Do buckle bodies deep into seats.
Out the windows, Earth is receding
into a collective memory
of how we were all held as babies.
With our hands over hearts
we imagine each beat aglow
like twenty fireflies. Our minds interlock
to form rotating haloes.
We venture in, to seek out new forms of life.
A hour on the page accelerates
beyond warp speed. I ask if they're willing
to believe a pencil equals power,
to write the truest thing that soars beyond
all clichés that pass themselves off
as a nice shade of green. Without need to worry,
we have no reason to defend.
Seconds before the bell, we've all disappeared
into the timeless where answers can't be graded,
where recess never ends.

KAREN BENKE
Poet-teacher, Marin County

Poem Is Banquet, Poem Is Feast

My students want to know
What makes good poetry?
I think, bread and potatoes, plenty of food in the cupboard.
A full stomach. Then vivid dreams. Attention.
Beginner's mind, I say.
Don't cross out. Take risks. Ask questions.
"How can one day be so many things?" one young mother wrote.
 A Zen koan I'm beginning to unravel.
Make desire statements.
This is the place I stop
To censure the thought (I'm losing my Buddha mind).
 No ideas but in things.
The thing is that truth set down on the page looks nothing
 like the mind of illusion.
The magician's trick. Sleight of hand. Not knowing.
But I want them to know, fully.
The way sky shines luminous
After July rain.
I want them to know.
Each word a jumping-off place
To ecstasy or sorrow,
Nothing in between.
A poem is a morsel to feed the hungry,
A grain of kindness.
Water that permeates
Unmovable stone.

MAGDALENA MONTAGNE
Poet-teacher, Santa Cruz County

In Search of a Poem

I am in search of a poem.
I decide to look in the world of imagination.

   Through a portal.
Across a bridge, over the river
Through a maze of hedges

In a dragon's lair
Over a mountain precipice
Through the fire world
By the sandy beach
   Over the sand dunes
At the gates of the ocean king's castle

This looks like a good place for a poem,
so I get out my pencil and start.

SEBASTIAN GARCIA
Grade Four, Dana Gray Elementary, Mendocino County
Marlena Nye, classroom teacher
Karen Lewis, poet-teacher

Haiku

This small bird
keeps batting against the window—
I rewrite the poem

TERRI GLASS
Poet-teacher, Marin County

Clouds Can Be Heaven

Remember when you were a river.
You are bored of being a river, then you see
water drops getting sucked up. You close
your eyes, and when you finally open your eyes
you're not bad, dark, bloody, injured.
You're white, healthy, happy—
flying because of the wind.

After years, you become a big cloud.
You see angels everywhere,
you see my father sitting there,
watching me write this poem.

CAMILLE DIEHL
Grade Three, Montecito Union Elementary, Santa Barbara County
Kathy Trent, classroom teacher
Christine Kravetz, poet-teacher

Once Birds

Near the window, inkblots
make a dark. Then winds blow clouds
north as flocks of once birds
flutter off shelves like dust.
The moon's eyes fill with tears,
afraid he'll never hear these stories again.
Wings disappear into the night.
Once, a very long time ago,
stars made the sound of water.

SALLY DOYLE
Poet-teacher, San Francisco

One Day in Workshop

I present a poem I love
just the way it is
and the class likes it too
and they say why don't I send it out
and I say I have, but
it's always been rejected with no comment
and I start to cry, right there in the room
and I'm mortified,
but I finally let it all out
how every breath I take is poetry
how poetry has saved me
how every word I write
connects with the deepest parts of me
and that *this* poem is *it*
and all at once the others shrink away from me
slap their copies of my poem down
lurch up out of their chairs and stagger backwards
staring in disbelief at the pages
which are now dampening, oozing,
reddening with blood that soon
drips and spills all over the tabletop,
the hidden fault line of my life
ruptured at last
my poem threatening to drench the entire room
with tears and blood
and though this has never happened in any previous workshop

someone turns to me and sneers
all this blood, all these tears—
such a cliché

GABRIELLE LEMAY
Poet-teacher, Ventura County

Waiting for You

Poems stay
inside of you
just waiting
to go through your arm
and out the tip of your pencil

Poems want to be used
not just as a jumble of words
but as a friend

Poems live with you
they follow you around
feeding ideas into you

Poems are in the waves of a beach
calling you, somehow
just watching you

Poems are
within you
expecting you
to find them forever

Poems live somewhere in the galaxy
waiting for you

SHELBY MALENGO
Grade Five, Washington Elementary School, Santa Barbara County
Sara Barr, classroom teacher
Kyli Larson, poet-teacher

The Origin of Cursive

Cursive's first curl unfurled from a free-wheeling Frenchman fed up with the stop-and-go straight line of the Metro, who got on his bicycle and twirled like a thread through the streets weaving with words leading him to his job as a printed-book proofreader where he'd speed-read until the words blurred together and his hand wanted of its own accord to be freed to unravel the musical twine from his mind out onto his snaky back roads of thought and the heart on wheels with words that could breathe and spin through spokes across cerebral spheres in a humming peal that made him feel like he was trying on and taking off layers of clothing one by one like one would peel an onion . . . tying and intertwining bows of sound thought one by one like one might ride an Etch-a-Sketch

BRIAN KIRVEN
Poet-teacher, Marin County

Ars Poetica

To a class of sixth-graders I bring
photographs of the universe.
A bursting cosmos in party colors,
green & purple Milky Way
swirling celestial light—yes!
Now close your eyes, my baby poets,
rock-a-bye, rock-a-bye, what do you
see inside?

Name it. This is your poem.

Poetry is cool water to a parched throat.
Let me have it, let me drink it up.

Poetry is a sleek machine with no unnecessary parts.
It is the sleek pelt of a wild animal you cannot pet.

Words bend trajectory of
random thought.

> To see what is next in line,
> the eye   must leave the first.

> What is glimpsed in the
> periphery
> is poetry

It is meaning distilled into emotion.
It is the ability to measure meaning
by the length of a cat's yawn.

Poetry is condensed language; it is not condensed soup.

Because I was born an orphan
   (although my parents didn't know this.
   Babies switched at the hospital.
   It happens all the time)
   I entered the world with the mark of a poet.

Because the heart is not made of glass
   it can be broken and yet not break.
    Poetry is the witness.

Poetry is the highest compliment of any art—a cinematographer
& ballerina have something in common with poetry
—as does the space between the lines in a
divorce agreement.

Poetry is a real come cry in a fake love story.
Poetry is a porn star with no makeup.

A poem consecrates flesh unto flesh
in a marriage contract
              or dust unto dust in the grave.

Because my first poem was published
when I was ten, "the horse in the cold
he's so bold" rhymed his way to a happy spring "when
winter is over he can play in the clover" & the pleasure
of seeing my poem in print still thrills.

Poetry offers an unblinking stare
into a commonplace world and still
finds distinction
worth mentioning.

              The smell of irrigation water & dry grass
              sends me back to the lap of the meadow,
              to the farm,
              the poor, tired old farm,
              to a time when I did not know
              we were poor.

To be a poet is to die many deaths.
The seeds we plant are scattered all over the garden,
who knows where they'll come up next.

This blunt earth holds rain like a cup;
long, deep roots tie us here.

Now close your eyes, my baby poets,
rock-a-bye, rock-a-bye, what do you
see inside?

This is your poem. Write it.

TREE BERNSTEIN
Poet-teacher, Ventura County

Rhyme for Lunch

I am a criminal.
Oh, terrible crime!
I ran clumsily home
and I stepped on a rhyme.

It was a small one—
most rhymes aren't that big.
It squealed as I squished it
and dirtied its wig.

I cried out in panic
and picked the thing up.
Its head was the size
of Barbie's teacup.

It squished up its face
and it stuck out its tongue.
When I asked "You OK?"
it turned red and it sprung!

It jumped up so high
I thought it was gone.
so I rubbed both my eyes
and I let out a yawn.

I felt something land
in the back of my throat.
You can guess what it was,
and it tasted like oats!

I swallowed it whole!
My throat's coated with slime.
and now I have to speak
that gross little rhyme.

LILLIE GRAY

Grade Five, Lynwood School, Marin County
Sam Murdoch, classroom teacher
Terri Glass, poet-teacher

Oh, the Glasses

All my glasses are self-determined. They suddenly grow
blurry or create scenes where there were none.
Children appear where there are no children,
dolphins leap across the hedge and garage,
electric eels send sparks through the closet door.
Forever I'm wiping my feet to scrape the camel dung and oily
grime from the auto racers in the basement. The twirling
hat-trick man spins into the bathroom as though
invited and empties his pockets into the sink. His coins
jangle like tambourines. Ham hocks hang from the
kitchen ceiling where hooks have never hung. When
lichens grow up my feet and legs, I swap glasses, but
mushrooms sprout as well and creep toward my hips.
Now there's a water park in the living room,
otters are backstroking 'round the floor lamps in figure eights,
plopping water onto the hardwood floor, soaking the furniture and the
quilt my mother made me last September. When asteroids
rush to Earth and hollow divots in my garden through the window,
slam, I replace my glasses with another pair. I see a
tortoiseshell cat sunning herself on a huge couch,
utterly still and making an odd engine sound.
Very different from me. I smile
when happy. Waking, she stretches and blinks,
examines her world and does not flinch from
yowling hyenas or the backhoe digging through the roof.
Zippers part the sky.

CATHY BARBER
Poet-teacher, San Mateo County

Color Is Mine

Red like sky at sunset
is my heart thumping fast.
White like the sweat
flowing down my back.
Eyes blue and clear with
some bare confidence.
I take my pencil to write
my poem,
and I feel color is mine.

DHANYA SETHURAMAN
Grade Four, Gomes Elementary School, Alameda County
Mr. Tsai, classroom teacher
Jennifer Swanton Brown, poet-teacher

Paint Me Free

Paint Me Free

Paint me with flowing free hair
And evergreen eyes.
Paint me in the freedom of the sea,
The salty air a sharp smell in my nose.
Draw me in a quiet sleep,
A blood orange disappearing beneath the horizon.
Imagine a soccer ball
Bouncing off of my foot into the goal ahead.
Paint me with pride so great, I feel like a kite
Soaring above the world.

ELISE GUERRAND
Grade Four, Montecito Union School, Santa Barbara County
Kim Konoske, classroom teacher
Lois Klein, poet-teacher

My Arms, Fingers, and Hands

My arm is as straight as a ruler
    but fat as Anchul's Gatorade bottle.
My arm is like a metal stick rotating a lot
    but as soft as very soft clay.
My fingers are little tiny things from a small
    tree flying over the keyboard.
My hands are like the sun, its rays
    are my fingers and my palm is the sun.
My fingers are like keys, they do all my buttons
    and unlock my door.
My fingers are like the rock blasted out of a mountain
    when workers are blowing up the mountain to lay track.
My arm is my timepiece, my watch relaxing on it.
My hands are like a Lego set finally complete,
    my fingers finally attached.
My arms feel like Jell-O when I am very tired,
    but feel like chainsaws when I'm energetic.
My fingers feel like a toy switched off
    when I sleep.
My arms, fingers, and hands all are
    important parts in my body, like
    ingredients in a cake.

ANIKET PANDA
Grade Four, Gomes Elementary School, Alameda County
Mrs. Orr, classroom teacher
Jennifer Swanton Brown, poet-teacher

My Beach

The pounding of the waves
is like the tiger
inside my heart.
What if
the ocean had no sound
and my soul was falling down
like an earthquake
inside the ocean?
At once
I washed up on shore
and found myself.

GEMMA AHERN

Grade Three, Kenwood Elementary School, Sonoma County
Cheryl Ghisla, classroom teacher
Arthur Dawson, poet-teacher

Untitled

I am a sun doing a salsa dance to the moon.
I am a puffer fish climbing a coral tree.
I am a bald baby growing little hairs.

LARA WESTBROOK
Grade Three, Glenwood Elementary, Marin County
Jenny Conte, classroom teacher
Lea Aschkenas, poet-teacher

Two Muses/Dos Musas

I have two muses.
Dos musas tengo yo.
One dark-eyed, *morena,*
pupilas como un tiro
deep as the shaft of a mine.
The other
la otra como la mar,
sea green, *de ojos verde claros.*
I have two muses.
Dos musas tengo yo.
One likes silver.
A una le gusta la plata,
como le contrastra la piel,
how it reflects her color.
The other, gold!
A la otra le encanta el oro!
I have two muses.
Dos musas tengo yo.
One sings to me in the key of G.
Me canta en sol mayor.
The other in E minor
la otra en mi menor.
And when we share between ourselves
sólo un suspiro,
one breath,
a compartir entre los tres
boca a boca
face to face upon my bed

encima de mi cama,
each whispers in my ear
cantos, songs that only I can hear
que sólo yo entiendo
but they insist I teach you
que yo se las enseñara.
Two muses
dos musas tengo yo.
One speaks to me in English,
la otra en español.

JABEZ W. CHURCHILL
Poet-teacher, Mendocino County

San Francisco y México

Aquí hay más seguridad que en México
Allá es muy peligroso
Aquí hablan inglés
Allá hablan español
Aquí es un poco aburrido porque no hay niños jugando en la calle
Allá hay muchos niños jugando

San Francisco and Mexico

Here, it's a lot safer than it is there
There, it is very dangerous
Here, people speak English
There, people speak Spanish
Here, it is a little boring because there are no kids playing in the street
There, many kids are playing

DIEGO RUIZ
Grade Five, Mission Education Center, San Francisco County
Lily Chow, classroom teacher
Jim Cartwright, poet-teacher
(Translated by Jim Cartwright)

What Remembers

My heart
remembers
the blood
quietly being
pumped
from my head
to my toes.
The seed
remembers
being planted
and watered.
The bell
remembers
singing.

JOY STILLMAN
Grade Three, Tam Valley School, Marin County
Karen O'Toole, classroom teacher
Karen Benke, poet-teacher

The Little World Inside Me

The little world inside me
contains the lyrics of literature,
a silent family of stones,
the beauty of snow—
contains each pulse of the heart,
square by square, a frenzy
of simple connections:
the standing sun, multitudes of joy,
trickles of treasure, the moon's
shimmering peace, wisdom
from every corner of the world.

MAYA RABOW
Grade Seven, Mill Valley Middle School, Marin County
Andrea Gough, classroom teacher
Karen Benke, poet-teacher

What I Love

I love my singing
I do not like my feet
I love my black hair
I do not like my hands
I love my nose it lets me smell
I do not like my thigh it does nothing
I love my mouth it lets me taste
I do not like my head
I love to dress up like a spy, it is so fun

LEEANNE COGHLAN
Grade Two, Yick Wo Elementary School, San Francisco County
Mrs. Yee, classroom teacher
Margo Perin, poet-teacher

Smiling

I roll my eyes to roll the moon.
My nose likes to smell quesadillas.
Pop! Go my ears.
My mouth likes to lick cupcake frosting.

ARIANNA ESTRADA PEREZ
Grade One, Washington Carver Elementary, San Diego County
Michelle Wasson, classroom teacher
Claudia Poquoc, poet-teacher

Hummingbird

I am a hummingbird,
small and colorful,
that is searching for nectar,
searching for love from people,
the flowers that I know.

DAISY DELGADO
Grade Seven, Anderson Valley Middle School, Mendocino County
Amber Mesa, classroom teacher
Jabez W. Churchill, poet-teacher

I Want

I want to be an original,
The book in a room of Kindles.

I want to last,
My well-worn pages here until you can't read my words.

I want to make an impression,
Staying in your mind,
Not coming out the other side.

I want to mean something,
Kept even after my binding is undone,
My pages torn,
Words faded.

I want to stay young,
Fresh, no matter how many times my story is read.

I want to experience,
For my pages to be turned
Over and over,
Each time uncovering something new.

I want it all to eventually stop.
For my book to be precious,
It has to end somewhere.
But not anytime soon.

I want my flaws to not matter.
To be insignificant.
To be nothing.
Torn pages,
Dog-eared corners,
Lost paragraphs,
Faded chapters.
Everything into nothing.

KIRSTEN IKEHARA
Grade Nine, Lowell High School, San Francisco County
Winnie Lo, classroom teacher
Susan Terence, poet-teacher

What Do You Fear?

The darkness, the light,
The end and the beginning.

Darkness because it conceals things from me,
And light because it exposes me.
The end because I might lose something,
And the beginning because I might ruin something.

Darkness holds evil things
That prey on me,
Hurt me,
Eventually kill me.

But light holds me.
I can't escape and
I am open to scrutiny
From the people I love most.

The end is hidden from sight,
Is impossible to predict,
And holds many questions.
Will I lose the people I love?

But the beginning looms right in front of me,
And can only start when I decide.
It holds many risks
To myself and others.
Will my decisions hurt the people I love?

I cannot banish the darkness,
Nor can I hide from the light.
The end gets nearer every day,
And not much is left to choice.
The only thing I can control, the only thing that matters,
    Is the beginning.
Will I ever begin?

LISA VIVILACQUA
Grade Ten, Colfax High School, Placer County
Danise Hitchcock, classroom teacher
Julie Valin, poet-teacher

The Gray Generation

How are we the gray generation,
the kids too slothful to move from our beds
to make a dream?

I am living our generation in colors beyond the spectrum.

The blues of bruised limbs and lungs
have hung from the ropes above all heads,
the reds of broken families pull,
tugging luggage between arteries
in hearts, splitting veins,
thinking how to sustain a perfect torn home.
Yellow sickened minds bleeding
through silver-razored thoughts;
elegant crimson ribbons plume from their wrists.
Ebony clouds storming through the insides
of the angered, cursing and coursing ways to reality,
breaking bones, bruising lips and ears.
Thick bubbling purples
and pinks spewing from fingertips,
pasted to canvas, streaked faces showing
them that there is more to gray
than black and white.

BRITTANI MILLANI
Grade Eleven, Ukiah High School
Michael Riedell, classroom teacher
Blake More, poet-teacher

I Can Fail Better Than You Can

I can fail better than you can.
I am the failure master.
I'm amazing at doing nothing.
The concrete is jealous
of my nothingness abilities.
I'm so insignificant
that all the little specks of dust
would do anything to be like me.
I'm so completely purposeless
that all the rubbish in the dumpster
cries because it won't be as purposeless as me.
I can fail better than you can!
Be jealous!
I'm the happiest failure on the planet.
The potatoes are jealous of my stupidity.
The sloths are jealous of my laziness.
I can fail so much better than you.
I'm proud to not care that I fail.
I think it's wonderful.
I will brag about it until the end of time.

I don't have any medals
or awards hanging on the wall,
but I have a bucket full of happiness
overflowing in my soul.

MADII BAZARD

Grade Nine, Redwood Writing Project's Young Writers Academy, Humboldt County
Melanie Nannizzi, classroom teacher
Dan Zev Levinson, poet-teacher

Right Side Up and Forward

(Read bottom to top)

truly here.
means you're really,
and backwards
To be upside down

I'd disappear.
not up, eventually
grow down and
If I were to

with your head first?
you burst, was it not
this crazy world
And when into

sun around me?
or is it the
the sun,
Am I going around

I see.
I wonder what
the sun from Earth
When I peer to

turn around.
home, they don't
go back to their
And when they

up not down.
sea, they go
come from the
When the waves

quite ideal.
it's really
think about it,
But when I

how I feel.
is sometimes
and backwards
Upside down

SOPHIA ROMINGER
Grade Twelve, Eureka Community School, Humboldt County
Marty Casillas, classroom teacher
Dan Zev Levinson, poet-teacher

Who Do You Think I Am?

Being black, you might think
Oh yeah, she's loud, hangs out with
The wrong crowd and
She'll be pregnant before she's eighteen

But you don't even know me
To be judging me

I am smart, love to read
And I write poetry

But those are the things
You wouldn't see in a girl like me

I am not who you think I am

You think that I have no dreams
That I'll end up spending my life in a penitentiary

But how are you going to crush my dreams
When your own daughter is going through the same thing?

How are you going to get to know me
When you label me as a stupid, good-for-nothing, bad teen?

But you don't even know me to be saying those foul things
I'm just saying . . . let me do me

LASHANAE BARNES
Grade Eleven, Ida B. Wells High School, San Francisco County
Dorothy Epstein, classroom teacher
Jean Teodoro, poet-teacher

My Mind

My mind is like a room
with memories
folded in the drawers
neatly.
My mind has answers
to tests
scattered on the bed—
then I don't know
what subject
they belong to.
Sad stories
are stuffed
in the back of the desk
and under the bed
trying to be
shoved away.
Nervousness locks me out
of the room
and sometimes
I don't have the key.
Guilt stops me
from getting out
with the truth
and makes me
throw out
a lie.
Most of the time

my mind is obedient
and puts ideas
where they are
supposed to be
so I can use them
when I need them.

VIVIAN HAN
Grade Four, Gomes Elementary School, Alameda County
Mrs. Simon, classroom teacher
Jennifer Swanton Brown, poet-teacher

Flying Swiftly

Free falling with no worries
The fresh air piercing through feathers
So many views wanting to tell different stories
Feeling the damp breeze that's changing the weather

Representing with pride and joy
Soaring through the sky
Asking myself . . . why is it so easy to fly?

We are the stars that lie upon daylight
Just as fluorescent moonlight lies on the night
The wind crashing, colliding
Against feathers like an ocean wave

Singing proudly very loudly
Shining bright like a speck of light
Spreading my wings as I start to feel alive

RAQUEL MACIAS
Grade Eight, West Marin School, Marin County
Ms. Cassel, classroom teacher
Brian Kirven, poet-teacher

California Poets in the Schools
Poet-Teachers, 2013–14

ALAMEDA COUNTY
Lilian Autler, Cathy Barber, Karen Benke, J. Ruth Gendler,
Terri Glass, Grace Grafton, Maureen Hurley, Tobey Kaplan,
Alison Luterman, Tureeda Mikell, Neil O'Neill,
Julien Poirier, Mara Sheade, Jennifer Swanton-Brown

BUTTE, GLENN, SHASTA & TEHAMA COUNTIES
Heather Altfeld, Susan Wooldridge

CONTRA COSTA COUNTY
J. Ruth Gendler, Maureen Hurley, Alison Luterman,
Laura Walker

DEL NORTE & TRINITY COUNTIES
Daryl Chinn, Dan Zev Levinson

EL DORADO COUNTY
Chris Olander, Shawn Pittard, Julie Valin

HUMBOLDT COUNTY
Daryl Chinn, Julie Hochfeld, Dan Zev Levinson

INYO COUNTY
Eva Poole-Gilson

LAKE COUNTY
Michele Krueger

LOS ANGELES COUNTY
Michelle Bitting, Juan Cardenas, Fernando Castro,
Nels Christianson, Tresha Haefner, Jose Hernandez,
Kirsten Ogden, Alice Pero, India Radfar, Jessica Wilson

MADERA & FRESNO COUNTIES
Diana Hallare, L. Anne Molin

MARIN COUNTY
Lea Aschkenas, Karen Benke, Duane Big Eagle,
Claire Blotter, Sasha Eakle, Kathy Evans, Terri Glass,
Brian Kirven, Michele Rivers, Prartho Sereno,
giovanni singleton

MENDOCINO COUNTY
Bill Churchill, PJ Flowers, Jasper Henderson, Karen Lewis,
Blake More, Michael Noriega, Dan Roberts, Will Staple

NEVADA, PLACER & SIERRA COUNTIES
Kirsten Casey, Chris Olander, Will Staple, Julie Valin

SACRAMENTO COUNTY
JoAnn Anglin, Eve West Bessier, Chris Olander

SAN DIEGO COUNTY
Christina Burress, Francisco Bustos, Brandon Cesmat,
Veronica Cunningham, Anna diMartino,
Shadab Zeest Hashmi, minerva (Gail) Hawkins, Aries Hines,
Jackleen Holton, Georgette James, Seretta Martin,
Joseph Milosch, Jill Moses, Johnnierenee Nelson,
Claudia Poquoc, Celia Sigmon

SAN FRANCISCO COUNTY
Jim Cartwright, Laura Davis, Sally Doyle, Claudia Dudley,
Kathy Evans, Grace Grafton, Kathleen Kim,
Dana Teen Lomax, devorah major, Florencia Milito,
Brenda Montaño, Brenda Nacio, Gail Newman,
Margo Perin, J.T. Teodoro, Susan Terence

SAN LUIS OBISPO
Michael McLaughlin

SAN MATEO COUNTY
Cathy Barber, Maureen Hurley, Terri Glass, Margo Perin, Emmanuel Williams

SANTA BARBARA COUNTY
Lois Klein, Christine Kravetz, Kyli Larson, Perie Longo, Teresa McNeil MacLean, Chryss Yost

SANTA CLARA COUNTY
Jennifer Swanton Brown, Amanda Chiado

SANTA CRUZ COUNTY
Magdalena Montagne

SISKIYOU & SHASTA COUNTIES
Beth Beurkens

SONOMA & NAPA COUNTIES
Molly Albracht-Sierra, Jabez (Bill) Churchill, Arthur Dawson, Claire Drucker, Iris Jamahl Dunkle, Jackie Hallerberg, Meg Hamill, Maureen Hurley, Kyle Matthews, Phyllis Meshulam, Blake More, Gwynn O'Gara, Kathleen Winters

VENTURA COUNTY
Tree Bernstein, Emily Clark, Geoffrey Jacques, Gabrielle LeMay, Richard Newsham, Mary Kay Rummel, F. Albert Salinas, Shelley Savren, Asher Sund

YOLO COUNTY
Eve West Bessier

California Poets in the Schools

Acknowledgments

ANGELS

Anonymous, Anonymous, Anonymous, Daryl N. & Phyllis Chinn, Ken Haas, Viggo Mortensen, Alvaro Peon Sanchez, David & Susan Sibbet

MUSES

Chuck Adams, Donald & Ruby Branson, Milton Chen & Ruth Cox, John Drexler, Edward E. Frey, David Gavrich, Daniel Meisel & Amy Wendel, Stephanie Mendel, Jim Nickovich

STARS

Cathy Barber, Nels Christianson, Courtney Nash Gardner, Jamie Jordan, Aaron J. Lewis, Karen & William Lewis, Sally A. Lewis, Phyllis Meshulam

LAUREATES

Elizabeth & Park Chamberlain, Kathy Evans, Mr. & Mrs. A. Lee Follett, Saori Fujitani, Alison Geballe, Megan Hinchliffe, Kelly Ilnicki & Mark Lambert, Suzanne Titus Johnson, Arlyn Miller, Gay Phinny, Susan & Andre Roegiers, Jean Schulz, Julie & Curt Stevens, Thomas Wanket, Peter B. Wiley & Valerie Barth

PATRONS

Laura Alonso, Beulah Amsterdam, Warren Arnold, Alicia Atienza, Richard Beard, Thomas Benét, Sandi Berger, Tree Bernstein, Valerie Berry, Michelle Bitting, Jennifer Swanton Brown, Joyce Bryson, Emily Carlson, Ingrid Carlson, Paula Cheng, Susan Chiavelli, Christina Ciciarelli, Eleanor & Francis Ford Coppola, Alina Cowden, Robert Cox, Katherine & Gregg Crawford, Matthew Curtis, Timothy Daniels, Albert Flynn DeSilver, Patricia & Ted Dienstfrey, Leagrey Dimond-Thidwick Books, Lee Doan, Paul Downer, Sally & Timothy Doyle, Terry Ehret, Sandra K. Erickson, Sharon Escott, Toby & Philip Flax, David & Vicki Fleishhacker, Sandra Florstedt & Bill Davidson, Sidney & Iris Frank, Alison C. Fuller, J. Ruth Gendler, Bernard Gershenson & Paula Gocker, Susan Gilardi, Dan Goodman, Kelly Gray, Andrew Hall, Jane & Kevin Hart, Brenda Hillman & Robert Hass, Meldan Heaslip, Helen Heinrich, Virginia Herron-Lanoil, Jane Hirshfield, Torre C. Houlgate-West, Debra Johnson, M.D., George & Sylvia Johnson, Tracey A. Jones, Louise Jordan, Barbara & Jim Jourdonnais, Linda Judd, Jane Kaplan & Donatello Bonato, Patricia Kaussen, Marci Klane, Eric & Katharine Kravetz, Suresh Krishnamoorthy, Jacqueline Kudler, C. Y. Leong, Rosanne & Alvin Levitt, Jonathan Lewis, Nina Lindsay, Peter Linenthal, Louis Lozano, Michael Lozano, Helen S. &

Leon J. Luey, Nion McEvoy, Suzanne Merner, Michael Miller, Diane
Moore, Elli & Tomi Nagai-Rothe, Gail Newman, Nancy W. Newmeyer,
Felicia Oldfather, Miriam Owen, Ruth Palmer, Tina Pasquinzo, Jeff
Paullin, Frances Phillips, Ira & Edith Plotinsky, Neal Powers, Barbara
& Nigel Renton, Scott & Marta Rich, Dodson Rob, Gordon Rudow,
Susie Schlesinger, Alison Seevak, Ted Sexauer, Ruth O. Sherer, Regina
Sneed, Kerry Sobol, Susan E. Stewart, Gretchen Stone, Jean Sward,
Roselyne C. Swig, David & Susan Terris, Frances Tibon-Estoista,
Melinda Wallis, Paul Whyte, M.D., Susan Wooldridge, Steven Wright

FRIENDS
Rhea Aguinaldo, Joanne Alexander, Leonard Anderson, Richard
& M. Natica Angilly, JoAnn M. Anglin, Emily Anicich, Corrinna
Aragon, Helen Margaret Archer-Duste, Linda Artel & Bruce Berg,
Lea Aschkenas, Marika Baire-Kark, Joan Baranow, Cynthia Barton,
Rick Barton, Ellen Bass, Judy Bebelaar, Karen Benke, Marlene
Elizabeth Benke, Eve West Bessier, Beth Beurkens, Richard & Paula
Biren, Claire Blotter, Barbara B. Bonadeo, Lorraine Bonner, Lynne
& Michael Braverman, Claire Bronson, Laure-Anne Brown, Christa
Burgoyne, Juan Adrian Cardenas, Sandra Carlson, William Carney,
Jim Cartwright, Fernando Castro, Ka Yun Cheng, Amanda Chiado,
Christopher Chow, Jabez (Bill) Churchill, Kevin Clar, Catharine
Clark-Sayles, Ruth Coelho, Judyth Collin, Beverly Coughlin, Susan &
David Courrejou, Paul Crabtree, John Dahl, George W. Davis, Laura
Davis, Arthur Dawson, Beth-Marie Deenihan, John Deheras, Sylvia
Des Tombe, Ed & Verity Dierauf, Ellen Dillinger, Leonard Dixon,
Willard Dixon, Darla Donovan, Claire Drucker, Marta Drury, Claudia
Dudley, Ann Duffy, Victoria Ehrlich, Gail S. Eisen, Joy B. Estudillo,
James & Dorothy Fadiman, Randall Farnes, Herbert Felsenfeld,
Nancy Ferraris, Carol & John Field, Oscar Firschein, Janet Fitch,
FLOCKworks, Stewart Florsheim, PJ Flowers, Leah J. Forbes, M. Fox,
Nicholas Frederick, Mary Freericks, Ellen Friedman, William Gainer,
Sherri Gilbert, Terri Glass, Robert Gnaizda, George Goddard, Warren
Gold, Kathleen Morgan Goldbach, Erica Goss, Janet Goy, Grace
Grafton, Kathleen Gumins, Susanne Haffner, William & Patricia
Hager, Diana Paula Hallare, Jackie Hallerberg, Megan Hamill, Margaret
Hamill, Heather Hamilton, Helmer Hamilton, Joseph H. Harris, Jr.,
Minerva Gail Hawkins, Jean Hayward, M.D., Anne A. Helms, Suki
Hill, Judith & Michael Hill-Weld, Julie Hochfeld, Ida Hodes, Christine
Holland, Jackleen Holton, Celia Homesley, Terry Horrigan, Jodi &
Gene Hottel, Maureen Hurley, Elijah Imlay, Molly Jackman, Maxwell
Jacobs, Geoffrey Jacques, Elaine James, Reini Jensen, James Jordan &
Catherine Lazuran, Samuel Jubelirer, Jo Ellen Kaiser, Eveline Kanes,
Tobey Kaplan, Muriel Karr, Bill Keys, Alex King, Brian Kirven, Lois
Klein, Marla Bastien Knight, Dr. Luis Kong, Christine Kravetz, Richard

Krejsa, M.D., Michele Krueger, Irmgard Lafrentz, Maxine Landis, Kyli Larson, Ann Lazarus, Kristine Lea, Eleanor & Martin Leiberman, Emily W. Leider, Gabrielle Lemay, Lisa Lethin, Daniel Zev Levinson, Sylvia H. Levinson, Justin Lewis, Linda Liu, Joyce Lombard, Perie Longo, Felicia Lowe, Catharine Lucas, Yvonne Lyerla, Susan Maeder, devorah major, Victor Margolin, Seretta Martin, Yvonne Mason, Kyle Matthews, Laurie Max, Frances Ruhlen McConnel, Michael McLaughlin, Robert McLaughlin, MaryLee McNeal, Teresa McNeil MacLean, Scott Meltsner, Florencia Milito, Adam David Miller, Marian & Philip Miller, Magdalena Montagne, Brenda Montano, Martha Moore, Blake More, Henry Morro, Jill Moses, Lesley Naliboff, Brenda Nasio, Johnnierenee Nelson, Michael Noriega, Gwynn O'Gara, Regina O'Melveny, Neil O'Neil, Jon Chris Olander, Vivian Olds, Irving Olender, M.D., Michael Allen Orend, Melinda Palacio, Senthi Palanisami, Kristin Papania, Steven Pascucci, Julie Payne, Margot Pepper, Francesca Pera, Margo Perin, Alice Pero, Petaluma River Press, Kathi Petrick, Judy & Daniel Phillips, S. Phillips, Sander Pick, Victor Pineschi, Shawn Pittard, Kumar Plocher, Eva Poole-Gilson, Claudia Poquoc, Yvonne Postelle, James Norwood Pratt, Katy Pye, India T. Radfar, Michelle Jenny Rand, Gail Rappaport, Toni Rinn, Dan Roberts, Teresa Roche, Lin Rolens, Sarah Rosenthal, Jennifer Rozenhart, Fernando Albert Salinas, Richard Salisbury, Ron Salisbury, Bruce J. Sams, M.D., Sasha Eakle Sanchez, Lewis Sargentich & Valerie Bradley, Shelley Savren, Dennis & Loretta Schmitz, Ingrid Scholze, Prartho Sereno, Mara Sheade, Eliza Shefler, Celia Sigmon, Allegra Silberstein, Murray & Marsha Silverstein, Pamela Singer, Livia Smoquina, Gary Snyder, Janet Sovin, Ivan Spane, Will Staple, Prudence Starr, Lani Steele, Hannah Stein, Mary Stein, Alex Steinberger, Richard Stookey, Joan Strawbridge, Wendy Swenson, Jean Teodoro, Susie Terence, Illia Thompson, Marissa Bell Toffoli, Maria A. Torres, Margaret Tsao, Allison Uba, Amy L. Uyematsu, Eloise Van Tassel, Nancy Warner, Al Weinrub, Karen Cross Whyte, James & Anne Williams, Janice J. Wilson, Jessica Wilson, Kathleen Winter, Sandra Wong, Mitsuye May Yamada, Patti & John Zussman

GOVERNMENT, FOUNDATION, & CORPORATE SUPPORTERS

Amazon Smile, the Arts Councils of Alameda, Humboldt, Lake, Madera, Mendocino, Sacramento, San Diego County, Santa Barbara, and San Luis Obispo Counties, The Association of Writers & Writing Programs (AWP), Barnes and Noble, The Blackie Foundation, Books Inc., The Donald and Ruby Branson Foundation, The California Arts Council, The Campbell Family Foundation, Center for Cultural Innovation, City Lights Bookstore, City of San Buenaventura, City of San Rafael, Communication Catalysts, Inc., Community Health Charities, Community Foundation of Sonoma County, Community Thrift Store,

The Companion Group, The Dougherty Family Fund, The Richard F. Dwyer–Eleanor W. Dwyer Fund, The Entrekin Family Foundation, Escape From New York Pizza, eScrip, The Frank Foundation, Frankie's Pizza, Gallery Bookshop & Bookwinkles Children's Books, The Garland Foundation, The Grove Consultants International, Harvest Market, KidQuake, LitQuake, Marin Community Foundation, Dave & Roma McCoy Family Foundation, Mill Valley Market, Inc., National Endowment for the Arts, PEN Center USA, Poetry Flash, Poets & Writers, Rotary Club of Mendocino, Rotary Club of Sebastopol, San Diego Border Voices, San Francisco Bay Railroad, San Francisco County Library, San Francisco Giants Community Fund, Sher-Right Fund, Dan D. Smith & Joan Marler-Smith Fund, Sidney Stern Memorial Trust, Target Community Fund, UCSF Benioff Children's Hospital, Ventura Community Foundation, Watershed Festival, The WITS Alliance, Woodward Family Foundation

Our Mission

Founded in 1964, California Poets in the Schools is one of the largest literary-artists-in-residence programs in the nation. We encourage students throughout California to recognize and celebrate their creativity, intuition, and intellectual curiosity through the creative poetry-writing process. We provide students with a multicultural community of published poets, specially trained to bring their experience and love for their craft into the classroom. CPitS serves more than twenty-five thousand students annually, in hundreds of public and private schools, juvenile halls, after-school programs, hospitals, and other community settings. We also partner with the California Arts Council to broadcast the Poetry Out Loud recitation program to high schools and audiences throughout the state.

To order copies of *If the Sky Was My Heart* and to discover more youth-publication opportunities, lesson plans, and poetry events, please contact:

California Poets in the Schools
1333 Balboa Street, No. 3
San Francisco, CA 94118
(415) 221-4201
www.cpits.org

Coming Soon to a High School Near You!

Poetry Out Loud, presented in partnership with the California Arts Council, the National Endowment for the Arts, and the Poetry Foundation, is a national program that encourages high school students to learn about great poetry through memorization, performance, and competition.

Poetry Out Loud is a natural complement to creative writing workshops.

To sign up your school please contact California Poets in the Schools or the California Arts Council. We are partnering to bring this extraordinary opportunity to all California high schools statewide.

info@cpits.org (Tina Pasquinzo)
kmargolis@cac.ca.gov (Kristin Margolis)
www.cac.ca.gov/poetryoutloud